Vanderbelt University   May, 1973

Reprints of Economic Classics

A DISCOURSE OF TRADE

Also in

Reprints of Economic Classics

By THOMAS MUN

England's Treasure by Forraign Trade [1664]

A

DISCOURSE

OF TRADE

From England *Unto the* East-Indies

Answering to diverse Objections which are
Usually Made against the Same

BY

THOMAS MUN

[*1621*]

REPRINTS OF ECONOMIC CLASSICS

A<small>UGUSTUS</small> M. K<small>ELLEY</small> · P<small>UBLISHERS</small>

NEW YORK 1971

First Edition 1621

(London: *Printed by* Nicholas Okes *for* Iohn Pyper, 1621)

Reprinted 1971 by

AUGUSTUS M. KELLEY PUBLISHERS

Reprints of Economic Classics

New York New York 10001

I S B N 0 678 00873 6

L C N 68-30534

PRINTED IN THE UNITED STATES OF AMERICA

by SENTRY PRESS, NEW YORK, N. Y. 10019

BIBLIOGRAPHICAL NOTE

A Discourse of Trade from England unto the East-Indies by Thomas Mun is reproduced from a copy of the original edition in the Seligman Library of Columbia University.

A
DISCOVRSE
of Trade,

From England *vnto the* East-Indies:

Anſwering to diuerſe Obiections which are
vſually made againſt the ſame.

By *T. M.*

LONDON.

Printed by *Nicholas Okes* for *Iohn Pyper.*
1621.

Briefe Notes directing to the
seuerall parts which are handled
in the Anſweres made to the foure
Obiections againſt the Eaſt-
India Trade in the Diſ-
courſe following.

The parts of the firſt Obiection,
Page 4.

1. IN *the firſt part is ſhewed the ne-*
ceſſary vſe of Drugges, Spices,
Indico, Raw-ſilke *and* Callicoes.

2, *In the ſecond part is declared the*
great ſummes of ready monies which are
yeerely ſaued to Chriſtendome *in gene-*
rall, by fetching the wares of the Eaſt-
Indies *directly in ſhipping from thence.*

page 8.

3. *In the third part, is proued, that*
the Trade *from* England *to the* Eaſt-
Indies *doth not conſume, but rather great-*

ly

A

A DISCOVRSE OF
Trade from England vnto
the Eaſt Indies :

Anſwering to diuerſe Obiections
which are vſually made
againſt the ſame.

He trade of Merchan-
dize, is not onely that
laudable practize wher-
by the entercourſe of
Nations is ſo worthily
performed, but alſo (as
I may terme it) the ve-
rie *Touchſtone* of a king-
domes proſperitie, when therein ſome certen rules ſhall be diligently obſerued. For,
as in the eſtates of priuate perſons, wee may
accompt

accompt that man to prosper and growe rich, who being possessed of reuenues more or lesse, doth accordingly proportion his expences; whereby he may yearelie aduance some maintenance for his posteritie. So doth it come to passe in those Kingdomes, which with great care and warinesse doe euer vent out more of their home commodities, then they import and vse of forren wares; for so vndoubtedly the remainder must returne to them in treasure. But where a contrarie course is taken, through wantonnesse and riot; to ouer waste both forren and domestike wares; there must the money of necessitie be exported, as the meanes to helpe to furnish such excesse, and so by the corruption of mens conditions and manners, manie rich countries are made exceeding poore, whilest the people thereof, too much affecting their owne enormities, doe lay the fault in something else.

Wherefore, industry to increase, and frugalitie to maintaine, are the true watchmen of a kingdomes treasury; euen when, the force and feare of Princes prohibitions cannot possibly retaine the same.

And therefore, as it is most plaine, that proportion or quantitie, must euer be regarded in the importing of forren wares; so must there also be a great respect of qualitie and vse; that so, the things most necessarie,

farie be firſt preferred; ſuch as are foode,
rayment,and munition for warre and trade;
which great bleſſinges, when any countrie
doth ſufficiently enioy; the next to be procured are wares, fitting for health,and arts;
the laſt,are thoſe, which ſerue for our plea-
ſures, and ornament.

Now, foraſmuch, as by the prouidence of
almightie God, the kingdome of *England*,
is indowed with ſuch aboundance of rich
commodities,that it hath long enioyed,not
onely great plentie of the things before na-
med, but alſo, through a ſuperfluitie, hath
beene much inriched with treaſure brought
in from forren parts; which hath giuen life
vnto ſo many worthy trades,amongſt which
that vnto the *Eaſt India* by name; the report whereof, although it is already ſpread
ſo famous through the world; yet notwithſtanding, heere at home, the clamorous
complaints againſt the ſame,are growne ſo
loude and generall;that (my ſelfe being one
of the Society it hath much troubled my
priuate meditations,to conceaue the means
or true groundes of this confuſion. But at
the laſt I reſolued my ſelfe, that the greateſt
number of theſe exclaimers, are led away
in ignorance; not hauing as yet, diſcerned
the myſteries of ſuch waightie affaires;Some
haue beene tranſported with enuie, as not
participating in the ſaid Societie, or beeing
there-

thereby hindred (as they conceiue) in some
other trade; and others, wholy corrupted
in their affections; who whilest they willingly runne into these errors, doe also labour
diligently to seduce others; that so, this
good and glorie of the kingdome, might
be subuerted by our selues, which by the
pollicie and strength of Strangers, cannot
so easilie be abated; wherefore, it is now
a fit time to meete with such iniurious courses, by a true Narration of the passages in
the said *East-India* Trade; answering to
those seuerall obiections, which are so com-
monlie made against the same; That so these
misunderstandings and errours may be
made knowne vnto the whole body of this
Kingdome, which at this present time is
most worthily represented in those noble
assemblies of the high Courts of *Parliament*;
where I hope the worth of this rich Trade,
shall be effectually inquired, and so in the
end obtaine the credit of an honorable approbation.

The first Obiection.

It were a happie thing for Christendome
(say many men) that the Nauigation
to the East-Indies, by way of the Cape
of Good hope, had neuer bene found

out; For in the fleetes of shippes, which are sent thither yearely out of England, Portingall, *and the* Lowcountries; *The gold, silver, and Coyne of* Christendome, *and particularly of this* Kingdome, *is exhausted, to buy vnnecessarie wares.*

The Answere.

He matter of this Obiection is very waighty; and therefore, it ought to be answered fully; the which that I may the better performe, I will diuide the same into three parts.

1 In the first, I will consider, the necessarie vse of the wares, which are vsually brought out of *East-India* into *Europe*; namely, Druggs, Spices, Rawsilke, Indicoe, and Callicoes.

2 In the Second; I will intimate the manner and meanes, by which the said wares haue beene heretofore, and now are brought into *Europe*.

3 In the Third and last; I will proue, that the Treasure of *England*, is not consumed, but rather greatly to be increased by the performance of the said Trade.

Touching the First; Who is so ignorant,

in

The First part concerneth the vse of *Indian* wares.

Sir. *Thomas Elyot* his Castle of health. *Rembert Dodoneus* his history of *Plants*. The *French Academy* second part, and others.

in any famous common wealth, which will not consent to the moderate vse of wholesome Druggs and comfortable Spices? Which, haue beene so much desired in all times, and by so many Nations; not thereby to surfeit, or to please a lickorish tast (as it often happeneth, with many other fruites and wines) but rather as things most necessarie to preserue their health, and to cure their diseases; euen as it is most notably set forth, by some learned men, who haue vndertaken, to write vpon this subiect; and therefore; it shall be altogether needlesse heere to discourse vpon their seuerall operations and vertues, seeing that, he that listeth, may be well instructed therein; if hee will peruse the volumes, which are penned by the learned, for the benefit of all those, who shall make vse thereof.

But if peraduenture, it be yet further vrged; that diuers Nations, liue without the vse of Druggs and Spices: the answer is, That either such people know not their vertue; and therefore, suffer much by the want of wares so healthfull; or else, they are most miserable; being without meanes to obtaine the thinges, which they so much want; but sithence I intend to be breife, I will insist no further vpon this point; For the Obiecters might aswell deny vs the vse of Sugars, Wynes, Oyles, Raysons, Figgs, Prunes, and Currandes;

Currandes; and with farre more reason exclaime against *Tobacco*, Cloth of gold and Siluer,Lawnes,Cambricks,Gold and Siluer lace, Veluets, Sattens, Taffaeties and diuers others manifactures, yearely brought into this Realme, for an infinite value; all which as it is most true, that whilest we consume them, they likewise denoure our wealth; yet neuerthelesse, the moderate vse of all these wares hath euer suted well with the riches and Maiestie of this Kingdome.

But I will come to the Raw-silkes and Indico; this being so excellent for the dying of our woollen-cloathes, thereby so much esteemed in so many places of the world; that for ornament, together with the great reliefe & maintenance of so many hundreds of poore people; who are continuallie imployed, in the winding, twisting, and weauing of the same; Insomuch, that by the cherishing of this busines (as his Maiestie, for his parte is gracioustie pleased to performe, in remitting the impost of Silke) it may well be hoped, that in short time, industrie will make the arte to flourish, with no lesse happinesse to this Kingdome, then it hath done (through many ages) to diuerse states in *Italy*, and latelie also to the Kingdome of *France*, and to the vnited Prouinces of the Lowcountries.

France and the Low Countries of late yeares do make great quantities of wrought silke, of which wares they were heretofore serued from *Italy*.

Now as touching the Trade of *Callicoes*,

of

of many fortes, into which the *English* lately made an entrance; although it cannot be truely fayd, that this commoditie is proffitable, for the ftate of *Chriftendome* in generall (in refpect they are the manifacture of Infidells, and in great part the weare of Chriftans) yet neuertheleffe, this commoditie, likewife is of finguler vfe, for this common wealth in particuler; not onelie therewith to increafe the Trade into forren parts; but alfo thereby, greatly to abate the exceffiue prices of Cambricks, Holland, and other forts of Linnen-cloath; which daily are brought into this Kingdom for a verie great fumme of mony. And this fhall fuffice concerning the neceffarie vfe of the *Indian* wares; In the next place, I will set forth the manner and meanes of their importing into *Europe.*

France, Italy, South Barbary, and other Countries.

The Second part Sheweth the manner & the meanes by which *Indian* wares haue beene and now are brought into *Europe.*

It is an errour in thofe men; who thinke that the Trade of the *Eaft-Indies* into *Europe* had firft entrance, by the difcouerie of the *Nauigation* by the *Cape* of *Good-hope.* For many yeares before that time, the traffique of thofe parts, had his ordinary courfe by fhipping from diuerfe places in the *Indies*; yearely reforting with their wares to *Mocha* in the *Red-Sea,* and *Ba'fcra* in the *Perfian-Gulfe:* From both which places, the Merchandize (with great charges) were after tranfported ouerland by the *Turkes* vpon

vpon *Cammells,* 50. dayes iourney, vnto *Aleppo* in *Soria*, and to *Alexandria* in *Egypt*, (which are the *Mart Townes*, from whence diuerfe Nations, as well *Turkes*, as *Chriſtians*, doe continually difperſe the fayd wares by Sea into the partes of *Europe*:) by which courſe, the common enemie of *Chriſtendome* (the *Turke*) was Maiſter of the Trade; which did greatly imploy, and inrich his Subiects, and alſo fill the Coffers of his owne cuſtomes, which he exacted at very high rates; But by the prouidence of almightie God, the difcouerie of that *Nauigation*, to the *Eaſt-Indies* by the *Cape* of *Goodhope* (now fomuch frequented by the *Engliſh*, *Portingalls*, and *Dutche*; and alſo attempted, by other *Chriſtian Kingdomes*) hath not onely much decayed the great commerce, betweene the *Indians* and the *Turkes* in the *Red Sea*; and in the *Perſian Gulfe* (to their infinite hurt, and to the great increaſe of *Chriſtian* trade,) but it hath alſo brought a further happineſſe vnto *Chriſtendome* in generall, and to the *Realme* of *England* in particular, for the venting of more *Engliſh* commodities; and for exporting of a leſſe quantitie of ſiluer out of *Europe*, vnto the Infidells, by many thouſand poundes yearely, then hath beene accuſtomed in former times; as I ſhall proue moſt plainlie by that which followeth.

And

[b] Rates vpon all ſorts of Spices. 22. per cent. Rawe-Silkes eſteemed about 2. per cent. *Indico* about 8. per cent.

And First, it will be necessarie to set downe the quantitie of Spices, *Indico*, and *Persian* Raw-silke (which is yearely consumed in *Europe*) and in them all to consider the cost with the charges to lade the same commodities cleare aboard the Shippes from *Aleppo*; and the like of all the selfe same wares, as they haue beene vsually dispatched from the *Portes* of the *East-Indies*; wherein, will appeare that happinesse,which many doe so much appose;especially our owne Countrie-men, vnder the gilded tearmes of the Common-wealth; whilest beeing indeed either ignorant, or ill affected, they doe not onelie grosly erre themselues, but also cause others to hinder as much as in them lieth, the glorie and well-fare of this Kingdome; but leauing them, I will set downe the said wares, in their quantitie and prizes as followeth; and first,

Such people as affect not the good of this Kingdome

At Aleppo.

	£	s	d
6000000. of Pepper, cost with charges at Aleppo at 2. s the P.	600000.	00	co
450000. of Cloues at 4.s.9.d.the pound	106875.	10	00
150000. of Mace at 4.s 9.d the pound	35626.	00	00
400000. of Nutmegs, at 2.s 4.d the poud	46666	13	04
350000. of Indico at 4.s 4.d the pound	75833	06	08
1000000.of Persia raw silke at 12.s the po.	600000	00	00
	1465001	10	00

The quantitie of Spice, Indico,and Persian Raw-Silke, yeerely confumed in Europe.

Now followeth the fame wares both for quantitie and qualitie at their feueral prizes as they are to be bought and laden cleare of charges.

In the East-Indies.

	£	s	d
6000000. of Pepper cost with charges in India 2.d ½ the pou.	62500	00	00
450000. Cloues at 9.d the pound	16875	00	00
150000. Maces at 8.d the pound	5000	00	00
400000.Nutmegges a 4.d the pound	6666	13	04
350000. Indico at 14.d the pound	20416	12	04
1000000. Persia Raw-filke at 8.s the pou.	400000	00	00
	511458	05	08

So

So that by the substance, and summes
of these accompts, it doth plainely appeare, that the buying of the said quantitie of Raw-silkes, Indico, and Spices, may
be performed in the *Indies*, for neare one
third part of the ready moneyes, which
were accustomed to be sent into *Turkey* to
prouide the same; So that there will bee
saued euerie yeere the value of 953543.l.
4 s. 4. d. starling of readie moneyes, that
heretofore hath beene exported out of
Christendome into *Turkey*; which is a matter of such note and consequence, that it
may seeme incredible, before the circum-
stance be dulie considered; and therefore
least I should leaue the matter in doubt,
it is requisite; that I doe make an explana-
tion of some particulars.

The exporta-
tion of the va-
lue of 953543.l
starling out of
Christendome
into *Turkey*
yeerely saued.

And principallie, it must not bee con-
ceiued, that this great aduantage, which
hath beene spoken of; is onely the Merchants gaine; for the Common-wealth of
Christendome, hath a very great part thereof in
the cheapnes of the wares, as shall be (God
willing) proued hereafter in his due place.

Secondly, the time of the Merchants
forbearance, and interest, is verie long:
his aduenture and assurance much dearer;
his charges of shipping, victuals, Marriners, and factors their wages, far greater,
then by the voyage into *Turkey* for the same
wares;

wares; ſo that the former great difference muſt be vnderſtood in theſe particulers; whereby we may perceiue to our comfort, that the Materialls of the kingdome, and the imployments of the ſubiects (in liew of readie moneies) becomes a verie great part of the price which is paid for the ſaid *Indian* wares; which cannot hurt the State (as ſome erroniouſly ſuppoſe) but greatly helpe it, as I ſhal better proue in that which followeth.

First therefore, I ſhew for an vndoubted truth, That the *Perſians*, *Moores* and *Indians*, who trade with the *Turkes*, at *Aleppo*, *Mocha*, and *Alexandria*, for Raw-ſilkes, Drugs, Spices, Indico and Callicoes; haue alwaies made, and ſtill doe make, their returnes in readie monie: for other wares, there are but few which they deſire from forren partes: ſome Chamblets, Corrall, wrought ſilke, woollen-cloth, with ſome trifles, they doe yearely vent in all, not for aboue 40. or 50. thouſand pounds ſtarling; which is no valuable ſumm in reſpect of that wealth which is carried from *Aleppo* and *Conſtantinople* into *Perſia* for Raw-ſilkes, when leaſt, 500000. poundes ſtarling *Per annum*: and from *Mocha* about 600000. pounds ſtarling (likewiſe yearely into *India*) for returne of Callicoes, Drugs, Sugar, Rice, Tobacco, and diuerſe other things. So here is ſtill a very great Commerce maintained betweene thoſe

Inſtance only, that ten ſhillings imployed in *Pepper* in the *Eaſt-Indies*, will require thirty and fiue ſhillings for all charges whatſoeuer to deliuer it in *London*.

The great Summes of money which the *Perſians* and the *Indians* carrie yeerely out of *Turkey*.

those Infidels; not onely for the Callicoes of many sortes, and other wares (which concerne their owne vse) but also for the Raw-silkes of *Persia*, which are altogether transported into *Christendome*.

How worthy an enterprise is it therefore in the English *East-India* Companie? by whose endeauours, there is now good hope to turne a great part of this wealthy Trade into *England*, by shipping directlie from the *Persian-Gulfe*, whereby the imployments, traffique, and Customes of the *Turkes*, may be still more and more impaired; & the generall Treasure of *Christendome* much lesse consumed; as is alreadie performed for the businesse of Spices and Indico.

The *East-India* Companie doe endeauor to bring the Raw-Silkes from *Persia* directly by Sea.

And who shall then doubt our want of Siluer to maintaine the Trade? if by this way wee doe obtaine the Silke, which with more aduantage and conueniencie, wil draw the money to this Mart, then it hath beene heeretofore conueyed vnto those remote dominions of the *Turke*.

And least peraduenture it should be thought, that the traffique in those parts by the *Christians* for the *Persian Silke*, is performed by change for other wares, or by the money which proceedeth of the sales of many rich commodities, which yeerely they sell at *Aleppo, Alaxandria, Constantinople*, and these parts.

The

The anſwere is, that neither the *Venetians*, *French*, nor *Dutche*, doe vent ſo much of their owne Country commodities in thoſe partes, as doe prouide their neceſſarie wants of the proper wares of *Turkes* : ſuch, as are the fine Raw-ſilke, made in *Soria*, Chamblets, Grogerans, Cotten-woolles, Cottenyarne, Gaules, Flax, Hempe, Fleece-woolls, Rice, Hides, Waxe, & diuerſe other things; ſo that ſtill the raw-ſilkes of *Perſia*, muſt be bought with ready mony. Only the *Engliſh* haue more aduantage then any other Nation in this kinde, for they vent ſo great a quantitie of broade-cloathes, tinne, and other *Engliſh* commodities, that the proceede thereof, doth not only prouide a ſufficient quantitie of part of the ſayd *Turkiſh* wares (which fit their vſe,) but alſo a proportion of about 300. great balles of *Perſia* Raw-ſilke yearely.

And if in any yeare, they chance to buy a greater quantitie of ſilke, then muſt and do they furniſh the ſame in ready monies from the *Portes* of *Marcellis*, *Genoway*, *Ligorne*, *Venice*, or the *Netherlandes*. Neither are theſe the onely meanes, whereby the *Empire* of the *Turke* is ſo abundantly ſtored with God and Siluer, to the performance of the *Indian-trade*. For, many are the *Chriſtian* ſhippes, which yearely lade with corne for ready monies in the *Archipelago* ; Great is the

Marcellis ſendeth yeerely to *Aleppo* & *Alexandria* at leaſt 500000.l. ſterling, and little or no wares. *Venice* ſendes about the value of 100000.l. and a great value in wares. The Lowcountries ſends about the value of 50000.l. ſterling monies, and litle wares. *Meſſina* 25000.l. in ready money.

the commerce from *Poland, Hungarie*, and *Germany*, with Gold and *Dollers*, for Chamblets, Grogerans, and other things : But that which is very remarkable, is the great quantitie of gold & ſome ſiluer coyned in *Grand Cairo*, which by two ſeuerall *Carrauans* (in bullion is yearely brought thither from the *Abiſſians* countrie in *Ethiopia*, for returne of many rich commodities, as Veluets, Sattens, Cloth of Geld, Taffaties, Woollen-cloath: poliſhed Corrall, and other things.

Thus by the coherence of the *Turkiſh-Trade* with the *Chriſtians, Perſians* and *Indians*, I haue ſhewed both the manner and the meanes, whereby the *Eaſt-Indian* wares haue beene heretofore, and yet are, in part, procured into *Chriſtendome* . But leaſt it ſhould ſeeme incredible, that the *Turke* would let ſo great a Maſſe of Treaſure yeerly to paſſe his Dominions, to the *Indians* and to the *Perſians* his profeſſed enemies: I will make the matter yet more plaine.

And Firſt, concerning the Raw-ſilkes, it is alreadie ſhewed, that hee hath the money from the *Chriſtians*. beſides the benefit he reapeth in their cuſtomes, with great imployments alſo for his Subiects. And for the Calliçoes (his whole *Empire* hauing litle or no other meanes for Linnen)he cannot poſſibly be without them, although it hath, & doth greatly exhauſt his treaſure, neither

neither doth hee gaine any manufacture by
the ſame, as the *Chriſtians* haue alwayes done
by the Raw-ſilke, to the great reliefe of in-
numerable poore people, ſo much prouided
for, by the pollicie of all well gouerned
and flouriſhing common-wealths; As by
this occaſion, and in a buſineſſe of the
like kind, I may inſtance the States of
Genouay, Florence, and *Luca;* who for the
maintenance of Artes and Trade, doe prouide Raw-ſilkes out of *Sicilia* for the value
of 500000. poundes ſtarling at leaſt yearelie;
and for the payment thereof they doe vent
at *Naples, Palermo, Meſſina,* and thoſe parts,
a certaine quantitie of *Florence*-Raſhes and
ſome other wares, for about 150000.
pounds ſtarling *per annum ;* So the reſt, being 350000. l. ſterling, is ſupplyed all in readie moneies; which treaſure they doe willingly forſake, to procure their Trade; for
experience hath taught them that Trade
is their imployment, and doth returne them
treaſure; for by thoſe ſilkes (being wrought,
tranſported and ſould at *Frankforde* and o-
ther Marts) they haue the better meanes,
to furniſh their contracts with the King of
Spaine in *Flanders ;* and ſo from *Spaine* the
Siluer muſt returne againe to *Italy .* But
if I ſhould runne out in this and other
particulars (fiting our purpoſe) it would
make me too tedious, and ſo carrie me
beyond

beyond my ayme, which is to be briefe.

Wherefore, I will proceede to cleare fome doubts, in thofe men, who perhaps not hauing the knowledge of occurrents in forren partes, might thinke, that neither *Venice*, nor *Marcellis* haue the meanes or yet the mindes, to exporte fuch great Sommes of readie monyes, yearely out of thofe Dominions; efpecially *Marcellis* being a part of *France*, where neighborhoode doth daily tell vs, that gold and Siluer, may not be conueied out of that Kingdome, for any valuable Somme, more then is permitted for the neceffarie vfe of Trauellers; Yet neuerthelefle experience hath likewife taught vs, that for the effecting of thofe Trades (whereof wee now fpeake, and which they efteeme fo much) there is a free extraction out of the fayd places, of moneyes both gold and filuer; whereof with them there is no want; for, the fayd wares doe procure it abundantly.

How *Marcellis* and *Venice* are furnifhed with ready moneys.

Firft, to *Marcellis*, it commeth not onely from *Genouay*, *Ligorne*, *Cartagenia*, *Malliga*, and many other *Porte* townes of *Spaine* and *Itally*, but alfo from *Parris*, *Roane*, *Sainct-Malloes*, *Toloufe*, *Rochell*, *Deepe*, and other Cities of *France*; who want not meanes to haue great ftore of Rialls, and Dollers from *Spaine* & *Germany*.

And

And in like manner, the *Venetians* diſperſing the ſayd Raw-ſilkes, and other wares into the ſeuerall States of *Itally*, *Germany*, and *Hungarie*, (who haue but few commodities fitting their barter or exchange: but onely monyes) are therewith aboundantly ſerued; For the mynes of *Hungarie* and *Germany* affoord good quantitie of Gold and Siluer; And likewiſe the States of *Itally*, eſpeciallie *Genouay*, *Florence*, and *Millane*, haue euer ſtore of *Rialls* out of *Spaine* in ſatisfaction of many great diſburſments, which thoſe Merchantes make for that King in his occaſions of *Itally* and *Flanders*; of all which, I might make a large diſcourſe, but I conceaue I haue ſayd ſufficient, to ſhew how the trade of the *Eaſt Indies* hath beene, and now is brought into *Chriſtendome* generally: what money is yearely ſent out; by whom; and the poſſibilitie, or meanes which they haue to performe it. I will therefore in the next place, ſatiſſie the *Obiectors*; that it is not the *Eaſt-India* Trade, which waſteth the Gold, and Siluer, Coyne, or other treaſure of this kingdome in particular.

The *Italyan Marchants* doe furniſh the king of *Spaine* with money in *Italy* and *Flanders*.

For firſt, who knoweth not, that gold in the *Eaſt-Indies* hath no ratable price with Siluer ? Neither hath the Siluer coyne of *England* any equall value with the

The third part doth ſhew how the *Eaſt-India*, Trade doth enrich this Kingdome.

the *Spanish* Rialls according to their seuerall prizes here, Besides that, his
Maiestie hath not authorized the *East-India* Companie, to send away any part
of this kingdomes Coyne either Gold, or
Siluer; but onely a certaine limited
summe of forren Siluer yearlie; which as
they dare not exceede, so neuer haue they
as yet accomplished the same.

For it doth plainely appeare in their
bookes; that from the originall and first
foundation of the Trade, in *Anno* 1601.
vntill the moneth of *Iuly*, *Anno* 1620.
they haue shipped away onely 548090. l.
sterling in *Spanish Rialls*, and some Dollers; whereas, by licence, they might haue
exported in that time 720000. l. sterling.

Also they haue laden away in the same
tearme of xix yeares, out of this Kindgome
292286. l. sterling in Broad-clothes, Ker-
sies, Lead, Tinne, with some other *English*
and forren commodities; which is a good
Addition, and vent of our wares, into such
remote places; where heretofore they haue
had no vtterance at all.

And note, I pray you, how time and
industrie, hath bettered this Trade, when
in the last three yeares, there hath beene
sent more wares to the *Indies*, then in
the xvi. yeares before; and yet our ex-
pectation

*How much
money and
wares the East-
India Compa-
ny haue sent
forth euer
sithence the
beginning of
this Trade.*

*The vent of
English wares
increased in
the Indies*

pectation is not at the higheſt, for thoſe new borne Trades within the *Red Sea* , and in the *Perſian Gulfe*, doe bid vs hope for better things, as lately by letters from *Spahan*, we vnderſtand of great quantity of Raw ſilke prepared by the *Engliſh* factors, which (by Gods aſſiſtance) wee may expect here about the Moneth of *Auguſt* next; with encouragement alſo, to vent our *Engliſh* cloth, and Kerſies in good quantities; the like of Iron, Tinne, and other things; whereof experience (of thoſe alreadie ſould) hath giuen vs ſufficient approbation of their valliditie.

And now (omitting much matter which might be written touching the diſcoueries of other Trades from one Kingdome or port to another, in the *Indies* : with the commodities thereof, whereby the imployment of our ſhippes, together with the ſtocke of money and goodes which is ſent out of *England* in them, may be much increaſed) I will draw to a concluſion of the point in hand; and ſhewe, that whatſoeuer Summes of forrẽn readie monyes are yearely ſent from hence into the *Eaſt-Indies*, His Maieſtie in the letters *Pattents* graunted to that Company, hath notwithſtanding with ſingular Care prouided, that the brethren of the Company, ſhall yearely bring in as much ſiluer, as they ſend forth,

Our ſtock may be much increaſed by Trade from Port to Porte in the *Indies*.

The moneys ſent to the *Indies* is all forren Coyne.

The *Eaſt-India* Companie are obliged.

to bring in as much money as they carry out of the Realme.

Tobacco, Ray-sons, Oyles, and Wines, whereof there is no want, but rather too much Smoake.

forth; which hath beene alwayes truly performed, with an ouerplus, to the increase of this Kingdomes treasure : Neither is it likelie, that the money which is thus contracted for, by the Companie at certaine prices, and to be deliuered them at times appointed, would bee otherwise brought into *England*, but onely by vertue & for performance of the said cōtracts; for, without this assurance of Vent, together with a good price for the said monyes, the Merchants would vndoubtedly make their returnes in other wares; the vse and extraordinarie consume whereof, would be found lesse profittable to the Commonwealth, when the matter should be duly considered, as I shall yet further endeauour to demonstrate.

And here I will suppose, That the *East-India* Company may shippe out yearely 100000.*l*. sterling; yet it is most certain, that the Trade being thus driuen, with such sums of ready moneys, it wil not decay but rather much increase the treasure of the kingdome: which to proue, I will briefely set downe, the substance of the *English* Trade vnto the *East-Indies*, concerning the quantitie of the seuerall sortes of wares, to be yearely bought there and sould here: with the vsual prices giuen for them in both places. And first, I will beginne with their Coste and charges

charges laden cleare aboard the ſhippes in the *Eaſt-Indies.*

In the Eaſt-Indies.

	l.	s.	d
2500000. ℔. of Pepper at 2.ẟ. ob. the pound ---	26041	13	04
150000. of Cloues at 9.ẟ. the pound.	5626	00	00
150000. of Nutmegs at 4.ẟ. the pound.	2500	00	00
50000. of Maces at 8.ẟ. the pound.	1666	13	04
200000. of Indico at 14.ẟ. the pound.	11666	13	04
107140. of China Raw ſilkes at 7.ẟ. the poūd.	37499	00	00
50000. of Callicoes of ſeuerall ſorts, rated at 7.ẟ. the peece one with another.	15000	00	00
	100000	00	00

All the ſayd Merchandize haue bin often experiéced, or bought at or about the prices aboue written; and we do hope for our parts (beſides the Trade of Raw-ſilkes from *Perſia*) yearely, to lade from the *Indies*, ſuch quantitie of the ſeuerall ſortes of wares as are here ſet downe (if it ſhall pleaſe his Maieſtie, to protect and defend vs concerning the

the Articles of agreement made with the
Dutch, that they may not violate any of
them to our hindrance or damage,)all which
wares in *England* will yeelde (as I doe conceaue) the prizes hereafter following, *Viz.*

In England.

	£	s	d
250000. ℔.of Pepper at 20.d.the pound.	208333	06	08
150000. of Cloues at 6.s.the pound.	45000	00	00
150000. of Nutmegs at 2.s.6.d.the pound.	18750	00	00
50000. of Mace at 6.s the pound.	15000	00	00
200000.of Indico at 5.s. the pound.	50000	00	00
107140. of China Raw-silkes at 20.s.the pound.	107140	00	00
50000. peeces of Calli-coes of seuerall sorts, rated at 20.s.the peece one with another.	50000	00	00
	494223	06	08

How much the kingdomes stocke may increase yeerely by trading to the *East-Indies*.

So that here would be our owne money
againe;and more, the somme of 394223.£.
06.s.08. d. aduanced towards the generall
stocke

ftocke of the Kingdome. For although the *East-India* company fhall difburfe the greateft part of the fayde fomme aduanced vnto his Maieftie for cuftome and impoft; and alfo vnto the Factors, Officers, and Marriners, for wages, together with the coft of fhipping Victualls, Munitions, Affurance and the like; yet all thefe (the Materialls of fhipping only excepted) are but tranfmutations and no confumption of the Kingdomes ftocke.

But if any man obiect, and fay, that the fayd commodities being brought into *England* (as is before written) they are either confumed in the land, or being tranfported into forren partes, they are changed into other wares; So that ftill we want our 100000.l. in readie money:

1 The anfwere is; firft, that in the occafion of this difpute, wee muft conceaue the fayd wares to be of no vfe for this kingdom, but onely for fo much, as doe concerne the Trade thereof.

2 And Secondly, in the faid Trade, wee muft confider, that although the faid goodes befent out, and returned home in other wares from forren partes; yet ftill, they are negotiated to the increafe of the faid ftocke, and for the imployment of the Subiects.

Laftly, if there be a refolution to determine

2500. Tonnes of fhipping wil lade home all the wares afore written from the Eaft-*Indies*. And the materialls of the faid fhipping (vnwrought) is worth about 15000l. fterling

India wares wil bring readie moneys into the Realme.

We haue no other meanes to procure Treasure but by Trade and Merchandize.

The *French* and the *Venetians* send the vallue of 600000.l sterling yeerely in ready money into *Turkey*.

mine and end the bufineſſe: who doubteth, that the whole value, may not be preſentlie returned hither in readie moneyes? For in *Italy*, *Turkey*, and other places, where they are moſt vendible to profit, there likewiſe is the money free to be exported at all times and by whomſoeuer.

And as it is moſt certen, that ſome other Merchandize, ſent out of this Kingdome were the meanes to bring in the 100000.l. in readie moneyes, which is here ſuppoſed to be ſent and imployed in the *Eaſt-Indies* (as aforeſaid) ſo likewiſe, there is the ſame power in theſe *Indian* wares, to procure other ſommes of ready moneyes, to be brought into this kingdome: For let no man doubt, but that money doth attend Merchandize, for money is the prize of wares, and wares are the proper vſe of money; ſo that their Coherence is vnſeparable. And if the *French* and the *Venetians*, made any doubt of this, they would not ſo willingly permit the vallue of 600000.l. ſterling, or more in *Spaniſh Rialls* and *Dollers*, yearely to be carried out of their Dominions into *Turkey*: whereof three quarter partes at leaſt are imployed, onely for the buying of *Perſia* Raw-ſilkes, which commoditie doth preſently enable them with readie money from diuerſe other States to performe the Trade; whereby their wealth doth much

much increase, and their people are greatly imployed. So to conclude this point, I will onely add, that the *East-India Trade* alone(although it be driuen in no amplier manner then is afore written)is a meanes to bring more treasure into this Realme then al the other trades of this kingdome(as they are now mannaged)being put together.

Trade maketh some States very rich which haue little other meanes.

For if the rule be true,that when the value of our commodyties exported doth ouerballance the worth of all those forraigne wares which are imported and consum:d in this kingdome, then the remaynder of our stock which is sent forth, must of necessitie returne to vs in Treasure. I am confident that vpon a diligent and true inquiry it wil be found,that the ouerballance of all our other Trades together will not amount vnto so great a summe of money as the *East-India* Trade alone doth ouer ballance in this kinde.

If the generall Trade of this kingdome doth export a greater value in wares then it doth import yearely, then doth our treasure increase

And to make the matter yet more plaine, whereas it is already said that 100000.l. in money exported may import about the value of 500000. poundes sterling,in wares from the *East-Indies*, wee must vnderstand that part thereof to bee properly called our importation that this Realme doth cõsume, which is about the value of 120000. pounds sterling yeerely. So the remainder being 380000. l. is matter exported vnto forraine

The trade to the *East-Indies* may be said to export 480000 poundes and to importe 120000.l. yearely. So the ouerballance is 360000. poundes sterling.

(d 2) parts

partes in the nature of our Cloath, Lead, Tinne, or any other natiue comodities, to the great increase of this kingdomes stocke, and that also in so much Treasure, so farre as the *East-India Trade* can be rightly vnderstood to subsist in this particular.

For as all humane actions haue their termination and endes, so likewise there must be an end assigned vnto the affayres of the *East-Indies*; which are then truely sayd to be finished, when this Realme is serued, and the remaynder of those wares which are sent from hence beyond the Seas, sould there and conuerted into money; which likewise from thence may be brought away freely & without the danger of Law or prohibition.

Forasmuch therefore as it is well knowne to many men, that monyes are thus procured by the Sales of *Indian* wares to profit, in the partes of *Turkey*, and at *Ligorne*, *Genoway*, the Netherlands, *Marcellis*, and other places: yet notwithstanding if all the said coine, or any part thereof should be diuerted from this Realme by some other new imployments or affaires, it must neuertheleffe be granted, that the sayd *India* wares had their finall end in moneies. But I will cease to heape vp any more arguments, to proue a matter which is alreadie made so plaine; wherefore leauing this Obiection, I will endeauour to giue Answere to the next.

The

Side notes:

Euery action ought especially to be considered in his ende.

The *East-India* wares which were sent beyond the seas, are sould and haue their finall end in money, which might be brought into this Realme in that kind, if our other Trades did not diuert the same.

The ſecond Obiection.

*The timber, Plancke, and other materialls,
for making of ſhipping, is exceeding-
lie Waſted, and made dearer, by the
building of ſo many great Shippes,
as are yearely ſent to Trade in the
Eaſt-Indies; and yet the State hath
no vſe of any of them vpon occaſion:
For either they are not here; or elſe they
come home verie weake, and vnſer-
uiceable.*

The Anſwere.

His *Eaſt-India* Trade ſeemeth
to be borne and brought vp
an Vnthrift, for it waſteth
and conſumeth all; Neither
doth it good to any.

But the Obiection, in ſome part is
verie weake:
And in the reſt it is miſtaken.

For firſt, concerning the weakeneſſe thereof, would men haue vs to keepe our woods
and goodly trees to looke vpon? they might
aſwell forbid the working of our woolls, &
ſending forth our cloth to forren partes ; for
both

The firſt part concerneth the folly of the Obiection.

both are meanes alike, to procure the neceffarie wares, which this Kingdome wanteth.
Doe they not knowe that trees doe liue and
growe· and being great, they haue a time to
dye and rot, if oportunitie make no better
vfe of them? and what more noble or profitable vfe then goodly Shipps for Trade
& warre? are they not our barnes for wealth
and plentie, feruing as walles and Bul-
warkes for our peace and happines? Doe not
their yearely buildings maintaine many
hundred poore people, and greatlie increafe
the number of thofe Artefmen which are fo
needfull for this common wealth?

The prouidence of the *Eaft-India* company for timber and Planke.

And is not all this good performed alfo
(with great prouidence) by bringing in
yearelie ftore of Tymber, and other prouifions from *Ireland*? Why then, where is the
great waft and dearneffe? I am fure, the *Eaft-
India* Companie findes it not; for whereas
they doe only buy their prouifions in *Hamp-
fhire*, *Effex*, *Kent*, and *Barkefhire*, in all which

The *Eaft-India* Trade hath not indeared the materialls which ferue to make Shippes

places they now may haue both Timber,
Planks, Sheathing boards, Treualls, and the
like, both for goodnes and price, as cheape
(yea better cheape) then they haue bin this
fifteene yeers; and likewife in all that courfe
of time their Bookes doe plainely fhew that
thofe wares haue neuer varied much; for if
they haue rifen any fmal matter in one yeare
they haue fallen as much the next. And yet I
pray

pray you obſerue (beſides the *Eaſt-India* Companies buildings) the many goodlie ſhippes, which are daily made for other priuate Merchants (ſuch as *England* neuer had before:) & that which is moſt remarkable, is, the continuall late buildings of his Maieſtie, thereby yearely adding more ſtrength and glory of great Shippes, to his *Royall* and matchleſſe *Nauy*; ſo that, here wee ſee this ſuppoſed waſt and want is not conſiderable.

Yea but, ſay they, the *Eaſt-India* Shippes are neuer here, to ſerue the Kingdome vpon occaſion: Or if they beat home, they are weake, and vnfit for ſeruice.

The ſecond Part ſheweth the miſtaking in the Obieƈtion

In trade of Merchandize our Shippes muſt goe and come, they are not made to ſtay at home; Yet neuertheleſſe, the *Eaſt-India* companie are well prepared at all times, to ſerue his Maieſtie, and his Kingdomes, with many warlike prouiſions, which they alwayes keep in ſtore; ſuch as Timber, Plancks, Iron-workes, Maſts, Cordage, Anchors, Caſke, Ordinance, Powder, Shot, Viƈtualls readie packed, Wine, Sider, and a world of other things, fitting the preſent building, repairing and diſpatch of Shippes to Sea; as may bee plentifullie ſeene in their yardes and ſtore-houſes at *Deptforde*, and more eſpeciallie in thoſe at *Blackewalle*; which are growne ſo famous, that they are daily viſited & viewed by ſtrangers, as well *Embaſſadors*, as others;

The warlike prouiſion which the *Eaſt-India* Companie keepe in ſtore

to

His Maiesties
strength in the
East-India
Company
alone.

to their great admiration of his Maiesties
strength, &glorie, in one only Company of
his Merchants, able at short warning to set
forth a fleete of Ships of great force&power.

For it is well knowne to al men who please
truely to be informed, That the *East-India*
Companie (besides their fleetes of Shippes
going and comming & also abiding in the
ndies) are continuallie building, repairing,
rigging, victualling, and furnishing to Sea,
with all prouision needefull for such a long
voyage, some 7.or 8. great shippes yearelie;
which are to be seene at an Anchor in the
Riuer of *Thames* in a great forwardnes some
5.or.6.moneths together, before they commonly depart for the *Indies*, which is about
the moneth of *March*: & they are no sooner
got off from the coast of *England*, but shortly
after, is the season of our ships to returne
from the *Indies*; who come not hume so
weake as some would haue them; for how often hath experience bin made of our shippes
which haue performed 2.or.3. seueral voyages to the *East-Indies*? Yet at their returne,
they haue bin indocked, new trimmed and
lanched out againe, fitted for the like voyages, in lesse then 2.moneths. But it will be
needelesse to spend any more time in shew-
ing the errors of this 2.Obiection: therfore I
will rather come to the handling of that
which followeth.

The shippes
which returne
from the *East-
Indies* home,
may be repay-
red in a very
short time.

The

The third Obiection.

The voyages to the Eaſt Indies doe greatly conſume our victuals, and our Marriners: leauing many poore widdowes and Children vnrelieued; Beſides, that many Ships are yearely ſent forth to the Eaſt Indies, and few we ſee as yet returned; Alſo, this Trade hath greatly decayed the Traffique and ſhipping, which were wont to be imployed into the Streights: And yet the ſaid Trade to the Eaſt Indies, is found very vnprofitable to the Aduenturers: Neither doth the Common-wealth finde any benefit by the cheapeneſſe of Spice and Indico, more then in times paſt.

The Anſwer.

Why, what a world of miſchiefes haue we heere ?

1.   ⎧ *Dearth.*
2.   ⎪ *Mortalitie.*
3.   ⎬ *Deſtruction.*
4.   ⎪ *Beggerie.*
5.   ⎩ *And neuer a whit the neere.*

A verie Teame of calamities, drawing on to miſerie; is it not then high time to ſeeke a remedie? yes verily, and it will be eaſily done, becauſe theſe euils neuer were (as yet at leaſt) procured by the *Eaſt India Trade,* as I ſhall ſhew, by anſwering all the parts in order as they ſtand : and firſt of *Dearth.*

It is both naturall and iuſt, that euery Kingdome, State, or Common-wealth, ſhould feede and cheriſh

The firſt Part concerneth Dearth.

cherifh vp the Natiue people of all degrees and conditions whatſoeuer, to their preſeruation of life and health, with ſuch meanes and moderation, as their plentie ſhall affoord ; and this is not onely due to them in the time of their aboad at home, but alſo vpon all occaſions of voyages into other Countries beyond the Seas, wherein they ſhall be imployed for their owne maintenance, and for the good of the Common-wealth.

The manner how the Eaſt India Company do victuall their ſhips.

Now therefore concerning the prouiſion of victuals (which in this Kingdome is yearely prepared for the ſetting forth of thoſe Ships which ſaile to the *Eaſt Indies,*) it is well knowen to many men, that it is alwaies proportioned, for about eighteene months ; whereas commonly the voyages proue a yeare longer, ſo that this ouer-plus of time, is furniſhed with the victuals of forreine parts.

And likewiſe for the Bread and Bisket which is ſhipped from hence, hath it not alwaies beene made of French Corne, purpoſly brought ouer hither (and that at a deare rate) onely to preſerue the plentie of our owne graine ? vntill now of late daies that the Farmers heere beginne to cry out and ſay, That the cheapneſſe of Corne doth diſinable them to pay their deare Rents : Thus doe the *Eaſt India* Company euerie way accommodate their proceedings for the good of the Kingdome.

And further concerning their Drinke, is it not a very great part water ? Some Wine and Sider, and but little Beere.

Alſo

Also the Flesh they eate, is Beefe and Porke, and that onely for three daies in a weeke; the rest of their victuals is Fish, some Butter, Cheese, Pease, Oatemale, and other things; all which is proportioned into a very sparing dyet to euerie man by allowance: so that heere is no excesse nor ryot, or any other meanes to make our victuals scant and deare, as is by some erroniously supposed; but rather by this course of life, our plentie is much aduanced. And so I will giue answer to the next part which is mortalitie and great decay of Marriners.

The life of man is so pretious, that it ought not lightly to be expoſed to danger; And yet we know, that the whole course of our life, is nothing but a paſſage vnto Death; wherein one can neither stay nor slacke his pace, but all men runne in one manner, and in one celeritie; The shorter liuer runnes his course no faster then the long, both haue a like paſſage of time; howbeit, the first hath not so farre to runne as the later.

Now, it is this length of life which Nature seekes, and States likewise endeauour to preserue in worthy men; but none are accounted so worthy in this nature, saue onely they, who labour in their vocations and functions, both for the publique good, and for their priuate benefit.

Thus may we esteeme our good Marriners, to be of no small vse vnto this Common-wealth: but take them from their laudable and accustomed imployments, for want of voyages to Sea; wee see what desperate courses they doe then attempt,

by

The Second Part concerneth Mortality

Good Marriners are accounted worthy men in a Common-wealth.

by ioyning, euen with *Turkes* and Infidels, to rob and spoyle all Chriftian Nations; fo that we may conclude, we muft not onely breed vp Marriners, but alfo feeke by Trade, to giue them maintenance.

Well, all this is true, but (fay they) the *Eaft India* company doth neither breed nor maintaine, but deftroy the wonted number of our Marriners.

How can this be, when it is moft certaine, that *England* (befides the *Eaft India* fleets)had neuer yet more fhipping then at this prefent? neither do any of them ftay at home for want of Marriners,no,not at this time, when many hundred Saylers are employed in extraordinary feruice, for his Maieftie in a Royall fleete of fhips, now at Sea: befides thofe great numbers of our beft Marriners, which haue beene and dayly are waited and taken prifoners by the *Turkes;* fo where is this want,or what is our mifery more then the want of true information in them that are fo ill perfwaded of our company?

Is it not certaine, that as the *Eaft India* voyages are long,fo likewife in Natures courfe many fhould die by length of time although they ftayd at home? And to recompence the loffe of thofe that dye,doe not the *Eaft India* company with great prouidence, yearly fhip out at leaft 400.Landmen in their fleets, which in one voyage proue good Marriners to ferue the Kingdome and Common wealth, vnto which many of them were a burthen before they obtained this employment? And thus is the Kingdome purged of defperate and vnruly people, who being kept in awe by the good difcipline at Sea, do often

The breeding of 400. Marriners yearely. Befides that the feare of a few mens death ought not to ouerthrow or hinder the performance of honourable actions for the feruice of the King and comonwealth.

often change their former courſe of life, and ſo advance their fortunes.

Neither indeed are theſe voyages ſo dangerous and mortall, as is reported; for how many of our ſhips, haue gone and come from the *Eaſt Indies*, without the loſſe of fiue men in a hundreth? Others againe haue had worſe ſucceſſe in the firſt beginning, when the ſeaſons, the places and their contagions were not ſo well knowne vnto vs; yet time hath taught vs many things, both for the preſeruation of health, and ſpeedier performance of our voyage thē heretofore. But the Method of my diſcourſe bids me write more of this in the next part, which is deſtruction; and this I muſt diuide into two parts.

In the firſt I will conſider the want of diuers ſhips ſent to the *Eaſt Indies*, which are waſted there.

And in the ſecond I will anſwer the ſuppoſed ouerthrow of the *Turkie* trade, together with much of our ſhipping which were wont to bee employed thither.

First therefore concerning the decay of our ſhips in the *Indies*, it cannot be denyed, but there hath been great ſpoyle of them in theſe three laſt yeares; not by the dangers of the Seas, or by the ſtrength of enemies; but by vnkinde and vnexpected quarrels with our neighbours the *Hollanders*, who haue taken and ſurpriſed twelue of our ſhips at ſeuerall times, and in ſundry places, to our vnſpeakeable loſſe and hinderance; together with the death of many of our worthyeſt Marriners, who haue beene ſlaine and died priſoners vnder their hands: and this hath ſo much the more encreaſed the rumour of their

their mortality: Neither lift I here to aggrauate the fact, more thē thus breifly to giue anfwer tothe obiection:for our late vnion with the *Dutch*,doth promife a double recompence of gain in time to come.

And they who make this Trade fo poore and vnprofitable,are much miftaken in the reckoning; for the prefent loffes which caufeth many aduenturers fo much to defpaire , is not in the fubftance of the Trade,but by the euill accidents which hane befalne the fame:& to make this pointmore plain,I muft yet declare fome other particulars : in which I will endeauour very briefly to fet downe the fumme of the whole bufineffe , which the *Englifh* hath hitherto performed in the *Eaft Indies.*

First, therefore I doe obferue that fince the beginning of this Trade, vntill the Moneth of *Iuly* laft *Anno* 1620.there haue beene fent thither 79. fhips in feuerall voyages, whereof 34. are already come home in fafety richly laden,4.haue beene worne out by long feruice , from port to port in the *Indies:* 2.were ouerwhelmed in the trimming there:6.haue beene caft away by the perils of the Seas; 12. haue beene taken and furprized by the *Dutch*,whereof diuers will be wafted, and little worth before they be reftored:and 21. good fhips do ftill remaine in the *Indies.* So this is a true account of our fhips.

And next concerning our ftocke , it is a certaine truth , that in all the fayde fhips there hath beene fent out in ready money as well out of this Realme, as from all other places wherefoeuer beyond the Sea(which hath not been landed in this Kingdom) the vallue of 548090. pounds fterling in forraine coine:

The fumme of the affaires to the Eaft Indies euer fince the Trade began.

Account of all the money and goods which hath been fent to the Eaft Indies euer fince the beginning of the Trade.

coine; and together with the sayd money there
hath beene shipped the vallue of 292286. pounds
sterling in sundry sorts of *English* and forraine commodities; all which moneys and wares amounting
vnto 840376. pounds, haue been disposed as hereafter followeth.

First, there hath been lost 31079. pounds sterling
in the 6. ships which are cast away : and in the 34.
ships, which are returned in safety, there hath beene
brought home 356288. pounds sterling in diuers
sorts of wares, which haue produced here in *Englūd*
towards the generall stocke thereof 1914600.ˡ.
sterling; for the charges arising here, is but a change
of effects from one to another, as hath beene sayd
before in this discourse: So there ought to remaine
in the *Indies*, to be speedily returned hither, 484088
pounds : neither can we conceiue that our charges
and troubles with the *Dutch*, wil haue wasted more
then the odd 84088. pounds sterling : so that I am
confident, that there yet remaineth 400000 pounds
sterling of good estate, for both the ioynt stockes.
And what a great value of *Indian* goods this sum of
mony may (by Gods blessing) shortly return in our
ships, which are there ready to bring thē, the example here doth teach vs to make vp the reckoning.
So that notwithstanding our great charges of di-
scoueries, our losses by the danger of the seas, our
quarrels & infinit hinderance by the *Dutch*: yet here
the kingdome hath and shall haue her stocke againe
with a very great encrease, although the Merchants
gaines concerning the two ioynt stocks will proue
but poore, in respect of the former voyages, which
haue not had the like hinderance.   And

356288. l.
sterling hath
been returned
from the East
Indies which
did produce
here towards
charges
1914600. ster-
ling.

There remains
yet in the East
Indies to be
returned home
from thence
about 400000
l. starling.

And thus in a few lines may be seene, much matter truly collected with some paines, out of the diuers volumes of the *East Indian* Bookes.

Concerning the decay of shipping and Trade into Turkey.

Now concerning the decay of Trade and shipping which were wont to be imployed into *Turkey*, I doubt, that in time it will likewise be affirmed, that the *East India* Company, haue hindred the vent of our white Cloath in the *Netherlands*, which to report were a verie strange thing. But (praised be God) to our comfort, we see the great increase of goodly Ships, daily built and imployed, by the *Turkey* Merchants with vent of more of our English Cloath (by one third part at least) then in times before the *East India* trade began.

Yea, but (say they) we haue lost the trade of Spices, and *Indico*, from *Aleppo* into *England*.

Well, I grant they haue; yet the Kingdome hath found it with more profit by another way; and they likewise are recompenced with a greater Trade, by the exporting from hence of the selfe-same commodities into *Italy*, *Turkey*, and other places: neither can it be lesse profitable for this kingdome, to turne the Trade of Raw-Silkes from *Aleppo*, and to bring them from the *Persian* gulfe, with one third part lesse money, then it doth now cost in *Turkey*; Besides, that by this meanes, the money proceeding of our English Cloath, Tin, and other wares in Turkey (not finding commodities fitting to returne for England) would vndoubtedly be brought home in Gold, as it hath beene performed heretofore, when by superfluitie of stocke sent from hence in Spice, together with our English wares; the

Mer-

The Turkey Merchants can and will iustify this truth.

Merchants (being thereby furnished with a sufficient quantitie of *Turkish* comodities) brought home the remainder of their stocke of those yeares in gold for a great value.

Thus doth it plainely appeare, that these reuolutions of Trades, haue and doe turne to the good of the Commonwealth; neither hath the affayres of the *East Indies* impaired or decayed any other Trade, Shipping or Marriners of this Realme; but hath mightily increased them all in it selfe. Wherefore let vs now take a view of this noble addition of the kingdomes strength and glory.

But this I must not doe, by setting downe the number of our *English* shipping now in the *Indies*, or lately gone that way; for they haue beene heaped thither, these three last yeares together without returne, saue onely fiue ships in all that time; the rest haue beene kept there to oppose the furie of the *Dutch*; but now we are at vnion, we shall (by Gods assistance) dayly exspect diuers great ships with returnes.

The strength of the East India ships.

And for the future time, this Trade I doe conceiue, will royally maintayne ten thousand tuns of shipping continually: (That is to say) going, and returning, and abiding there in the *Indies*; which said shipping will employ two thousand and fiue hundred Marriners at least; and the building with the repayring of the sayde ships, here at home will set to worke fiue hundred men, Carpenters, Cawkers, Caruers, Ioiners, Smiths, & other laborers, besides many officers; and about 120. Factors, in seuerall places of of the *Indies*. And so from these matters of great consequence, I must beginne to write of Beggery.

The pouertie of Widdowes and Fatherlesse is matter of great compassion, and doth alwaies moue Christian hearts to commiseration and charitie; whereby many receiue reliefe & helpe of those whō God hath blessed with better meanes: but how this pouertie should totally be preuented, it seemeth not onely difficult, but altogether impossible: For besides the euill accidents and miseries, which euer attend on our humanity, we see how many dayly (euen through their owne folly & wilfulnesse) do as it were desperately plunge themselues into aduersitie. And thus the number of those is great, who hauing the charge of wife & children, are notwithstanding altogether without meanes and artes to procure their maintenance; whereby some of them wanting grace, do run a desperat course, & haue vntimely ends. Others again, being better inspired, seek for imployment, but find it not, or with great difficulty: for, who doth willingly entertain a man poore and miserable, charged with a family, and peraduenture debauched in conditions? Neither doe any of our other Merchants voyages to forraine parts accept of those nouices who neuer haue been vsed to the Sea: So that when all the other doores of charitie are shut the *East India* gates stand wide open to receiue the needy and the poore, giuing them good entertainment with two Moneths wages before hand to make their neeedfull prouisions for the voyage : And in the time of their absence, there is likewise payd vnto their wiues for maintenance, two other

The fourth Part concernes the pouerty of widdowes, &c.

The East India Trade doth employ many poore men, & deboist people which other trades refuse

Wages before hand is not giuen in other Merchants voyages, neither yet so great wages as the East India company pay.

other months wages vpon accompt of euery yeares
seruice: and also if any chance to dye in the voyage,
the wife receiueth all that is found due vnto her
husband (if hee doe not otherwise dispose it by
will:) and this often happeneth to be more money
then euer they had of their owne together in any
one time.

And likewise, are not many poore Widdowes,
Wiues and Children of *Blacke-wall*, *Lime-house*,
Ratcliffe, *Shadwell*, and *wapping*, often relieued by
the *East India* company with whole Hogsheads of
good Biefe and Porke, Bisket and doales of ready
money? Are not diuers of their children set on
worke to picke Okam, & other labours fitting their
age and capacitie? What might I not say of repayring of Churches, maintenance of some yong
Schollers, relieuing of many poore Preachers of
the Gospell yearely with good summes of money;
and diuers other acts of charitie, which are by them
religiously performed, euen in the times now of
their worst fortunes? for all which I hope there shal
be a reward vnto them and theirs. And so I come to
the fift part of this third Obiection.

And here I must intimate how much they are de-
ceiued who thinke that Spices and Indico are no
better cheape in *England* now, then in times past,
before the *East India* trade began.

For, it is an vndoubted truth, that in those dayes
we often payd 6. shillings or more for a pound of
Pepper, and seldome or neuer lesse then three shillings and sixe pence the pound; whereas since the
Trade hath come directly from the *Indies*, it hath
been)

When did any of these wid-dowes beg for reliefe in our Churches as others often doe?

The East India company their charity.

The fift Part concerneth the cheapnesse of Spice and Indico at this present in respect of former times.

beene bought commonly at feuerall prices betweene 16.pence and two fhillings the pound; but
I will make the difference of price appeare more
plainely by fetting downe the quantities of Spices
and Indico, which are yearely fpent in the Realme
of *England*, together with the loweft prices, which
they were wont to fell at, when wee brought them
from *Turkey* and *Lixborne*; and the like concerning
their vfuall prices now that wee bring them from
the *Eaft Indies* directly; And firft as from *Turkey*.

Prices of fpice
and Indico in
former times.

400000.^{l}.of Pepper at 3 ^{s}.6.^{d}.the^l.70000.^{l}.00.^{s}.00^d
40000. of Cloues at 8.^{s}. the pound.16000-00-00.
20000. of Maces at 9. ^{s}.the pound.9000--00--00.
160000.of Nutmegs at 4.^{s}.6.^{d}the^l.36000-00--00
150000. of Indico at 7.^{s}.the pound.52500-00-00.

183500--00--00

And the felfe fame quantity and forts of wares
are commonly fold at the prices here vnder written
now in thefe later times.

Prices of fpice
and Indico in
thefe later
times.

400000.^{l}.of Pepper at 20 ^{d}.the^l.33333.^{l}.06.^{s}.08.^{d}
40000.of Cloues at 6^d.the pound.12000-00-00.
20000. of Maces at 6. ^{s} the pound. 6000-00-00.
160000.of Nutmegs at 2.^{s}.6.^{d}the^l.20000--00--00
150000. of Indico at 5.^{s}. pound. 37000--00--00.

108333.--06--08

So that this Trade in Spice and Indico onely, doth saue the Kingdome yearly 74966.ˡ. 13.ˢ.04.ᵈ. which is a matter worthy to be obserued; and so much the rather, becaufe it is a certaine truth, that leffe then a quarter part of this fum of mony which is thus faued yearely, fhall buy in the *Indies* the full quantitie of all the feuerall forts of wares before written, which doe ferue for a yeares prouifion for this Realme of *England*; but ftill, it muft be remembred, that the cuftome, impoft, wages, victuals, fhipping, and other charges (which are to be added) wilbe a greater fumme, then the mony which is paid for thefe wares in the *Indies*; but as I haue noted before, the faid charges doe not confume the Kingdomes ftocke, although it doth greatly abate the Merchants gaine.

And to conclude this point, I will adde vnto that which hath beene faid; that the commodities onely which we now fend yearely into the *Eaſt Indies* and *Perſia*, are of fufficient value there to returne vs *Indico*, *Spices*, *Drugs*, and all other forts of *Indian* wares, (*Raw-Silkes* of *Perſia* only excepted) for one yeares confume, or more in this Kingdome; So that now all the money which is fent forth in our Ships doth procure an ouer-plus of the faid wares to the furtherance of Trade from *India* hither, and after from hence to forreine parts againe, to the great imployment of the Subiects, and inriching of this Realme, both in Stocke and Treafurie; all which is matter very worthy to be diligently obferued; And fo I come to giue anfwere vnto the fourth and laft Obiection.

The

Leffe then 18. thoufand pounds fterling in the Indies, will buy Spice and Indico to ferue this Realme for a yeare, which is not halfe fo much money as it fpendeth beyond the feas to buy Currans onely, or to buy Tobacco.

The wares only which are fent out of this kingdome into the Eaſt Indies are of fufficient value to furnifh this Realme with an ouer-plus of al manner of Indian wares (Perfian Raw-Silkes only excepted)

The fourth Objection.

It is generally obserued that his Maiesties Mint hath had but little imployment euer sithence the East India Trade began; wherefore it is manifest, that the onely remedie for this, and so many euils besides, is to put downe this Trade: For what other remedie can there be for the good of the Common-wealth?

The Answer.

This fourth objection may be deuided into three parts:

1. { *An euill declared.*
2. { *A remedie propounded.*
3. { *And counsell demaunded.*

And first concerning the Euill or want of Siluer, I thinke it hath beene, and is a generall disease of all Nations, and so will continue vntill the end of the world; for poore and rich complaine they neuer haue enough:but it seemeth the maladie is growen mortall here with vs, and therefore it cries out for remedie: Well,I hope it is but imagination maketh vs sicke, when all our parts be sound and strong; For who knoweth not the inestimable treasure of this Kingdome in Plate possessed by the people thereof almost of all degrees; in such measure, as neuer hath beene seene in former ages?

And for his Maiesties Mint, it is well knowne, that there hath beene coyned in fiue yeares toge-

The first Part concerneth his Maiesties Mint

25000.pounds waight at least of Siluer yeare-ly melted down into Plate, be-sides old Plate new fashioned, as by credible report.

ther

ther since the *East India* Company began, 6214. pounds waight of Gold, and 311384. pound waight of sterling Money; all which Gold and Siluer doe amount vnto the summe of 1213850. pounds of sterling Money; How then doth this Trade turne the currant and imployment of the Mint?

But vpon the sight of this truth, perhaps it will be said, That wee must resort vnto the present times, (the Mint being idle now.)

To which I answer, That likewise the Mint had little or no imployment for coynage of Siluer in former times, when the said Company did not export aboue fifteene or twenty thousand pounds sterling at the most *per annum*; no, nor yet in the yeares 1608. and 1612 : when in the former they shipped out but 6000. l. -- 00. s. -- 00 d. and in the latter, but 1250. l. -- 00. s. -- 00. d. sterling. So that both waies we see, that the Mint hath had very great imployment fiue yeares together, sithence the *East India Trade* began; and also it hath beene without imployment diuers yeares, when the *East India* Company haue sent away but very small summes of money; wherefore of necessitie there must be some other causes and meanes whereby our Siluer is not exported onely, but also it is not imported into the Realme as in former times. For we haue not had the meanes by our owne plentie, nor by the scarsitie of our neighbours, (for the space of the last foureteene yeares together) to send out hundreds of Ships laden with Corne, as in times past which was returned home in Siluer; but

There hath bin coyned great store of Gold & Siluer in his Maiesties Mint since the East India Trade began.

There hath bin little or no Siluer coyned in some yeares, when the East India Company sent out very small sums of money.

but rather of late yeares (as is much to be feared)
a great quantitie of our money hath beene carried
out of the Kingdome, for that Corne which hath
beene brought vs from the East Countries, and o-
ther places, to supply our wants. Thus times doe
change, and our fortunes change with them: neither list I to make this matter plaine, by setting
downe those meanes, which heretofore brought
vs store of money, euen out of *France* and other
places, which now are ceased. But without any further medling in the Mint, I will come to the remedie which some propound, by putting downe
the *East India* Company.

But heere our comfort is, that the Obiectors are
not our Iudges, whose wiledome and integritie la-
bouring for the honour of his Maiestie, and the
good of his Kingdome, will soone perceiue the
mischiefes of this supposed remedie. And that the
pretended euill which many with malice chase, is
that great good, which other Nations seeke by
pollicie and strength to keepe, and likewise to obtaine; In which proceedings, it concerneth vs, especially to obserue the diligences and practises of
the *Dutch*; who with more gladnesse would vnder-
take the whole Trade to the *East Indies*, then with
any reason we can abandon that part thereof, which
we now enioy; neither can our restraint from the
Indies keepe our Siluer from thence, as long as the
Dutch goe thither: for we know, that deuices want
not to furnish such designes; and when their Ships
returne from *India*, shall not our Siluer out againe
to helpe to pay a double price, or what they please,

                                      for

Some causes and meanes which were wont to bring siluer into the Realme, are ceased at this present time.

The Second Part concerneth the putting downe of the East India Trade.

The East-India Trade is greatly desired by other Christian Nations

for all thofe wares which we fhall want for our ne-
ceffities?

Thus fhould the Dutch increafe their honour,
wealth and ftrength, whileft we abate, grow poore
and weake at Sea for want of Trade ; and call you
this a Remedie ; no, rather tearme it Ruine, Deftruction, or what you lift ; And fo I come vnto
the conclufion or laft part.

And here I muft confeffe my felfe aground, for
this matter is much too high for my handling : befides, my excufe is faire, hauing alreadie done my
taske to cleare the *Eaft India Trade* from imputati-
on ; the which, for want of learning, although I
haue performed, without varietie of words or
eloquence : yet it is done with all integritie of
truth, in euery particular, as I fhall be readie to
make proofe vpon all occafions, which may bee
offered.

And yet before I make an end, although I cannot
fatisfie euery mans defire, in fuch meafure as is neceffarie : yet I thinke it not amiffe to performe the
fame fo farre as I am able by common practife, and
my obferuations in the Trade of Merchandize,
which is my profeffion.

And firft therefore, all men doe know, that the
riches or fufficiencie of euery Kingdome, State, or
Common-wealth, confifteth in the poffeffion
of thofe things, which are needfull for a ciuill
life.

This fufficiency is of two forts : the one is naturall, and proceedeth of the Territorie it felfe :
the

(marginal notes)

The Dutch might grow ftrong and rich by our deftruction.

The Third Part concerneth the councel which the Obiecters demaund.

The riches of a Kingdome is of two forts.

the other is artificiall, and dependeth on the industry of the Inhabitants.

The Realme of *England* (praised be God) is happily possessed of them both: as first, hauing great plentie of naturall riches, both in the Sea for Fish, & on the Land for Wooll, Cattle, Corne, Lead, Tin, Iron, and many other things for food, Rayment & Munition; infomuch, that vpon strickt tearmes of need, this land may liue without the help of any other Nation.

But to liue well, to flourish and grow rich, we must finde meanes, by Trade to vent our superfluities; therewith to furnish and adorne vs with the Treasure and those necessarie wares, which forreine Nations doe afford: and here industrie must begin to play his part, not onely to increase and guide the Trades abroad; but also to maintaine and multiply the Arts at home: for when either of these faile, or are not effected with such skill as their mysterie shall require, then doth the Commonwealth abate & growes poore; neither is this easily perceiued at first, vntill some euill accidents doe stirre vp our diligence to search out the true causes, that so they being remoued, the effects may cease. And this is the subiect of our discourse which we now pursue.

This kind of industry maketh some Countries which are poor in themselues, to grow rich and strong by other Nations, who haue greater meanes, and are lesse industrious.

That which I haue hitherto deliuered, hath beene altogether Negatiue, still defending and prouing by arguments, that the *East India Trade* hath not hurt this Common-wealth; And now changing my stile, I must affirme as fast the true causes of those euils which we seeke to chase away.

These

These causes then (as I conceiue) are principally foure.

1. The first is the breach of Entercourse by forraine Nations.

2. The second is the abuse of the exchanges betwixt vs and other Countries.

3. The third is neglect of dutie in some Subiects.

4 The fourth is our dammage in Commerce with Strangers.

Now concerning all these, I might make a very large discourse; but my purpose is only to explane the meaning of euery point in order, as briefly as I can.

And first for the breach of Entercourse; by this I vnderstand those Nations, who haue eyther debased their Standard, or else ouer-valued the price of their Coynes from that equiualence which formerly they had with the Standard and Moneys of this Realme; And also doe tollerate, not onely their owne Moneys, but also the Coyne of other Countries (and especially of this Kingdome) to bee currant with them at higher rates, then the prizes of the Exchange; by which courses (being directly against the Entercourse) there is a greater cause giuen of exportation of the Moneys of this Realme, then otherwise there would be. For although this is done with great danger to the exporters of the same, (it being an acte against the Law of the Land) yet notwithstanding Couetous-

Foure Principall Causes which carry away our Gold and Siluer.

The First Cause concerneth the Standard.

Proceedings against entercourse.

uetoufnefle, being euer conuerfant in wicked
actions, thinketh nothing vnlawfull, which pro-
mifeth a certaine gaine; and how to remedie this
euill practife I finde it not eafie. For the debafing
of the Coyne, or raifing the price thereof in this
Realme, would much impouerifh the eftates of
particular men, and yet in the conclufion, would
proue a bufineffe without end: for who doth not
conceiue that which would follow beyond the
Seas vpon any fuch alteration here with vs? fo that
ftill the euill will remaine, vntill we find fome other
remedie.

And for the exchanges of money, vfed betwixt Nations, although the true vfe thereof, is
a very lawdable and neceffarie practife, for the
accommodating of Merchants affaires, and fur-
nifhing of Trauellers in their occafions, without the tranfporting of Coyne from one State to
another, with danger and loffe, both to the
publique and priuate wealth; yet is the abufe
thereof verie preiudiciall vnto this Kingdome
in particuler; whileft in the interim the benefit
doth arife vnto other Countries, who diligently
obferuing the prizes whereby the monies bee ex-
changed, may take aduantage, to carrie away
the Gold and Siluer of this Realme at thofe times,
when the rate of our fterling money (in Exchange)
is vnder the value of that Standard, vnto which
place they are conueyed; For in refpect the prizes of the Exchanges, doe rife and fall according
to the plentie or fcarfitie of money, which is to be

taken

The Second
Caufe concer-
neth the Ex-
changes of
moneys with
forreine Coun-
tries.

The practife
of thofe ftran-
gers here in
this Realme,
who make a
Trade by Ex-
change of mo-
neys.

taken vp or deliuered out, the exchange is hereby become rather a Trade for some great monyed men, then a furtherance and accomodation of reall Trade to Merchants, as it ought to be in the true vse thereof.

And thus many times money may be made ouer hither by strangers, to a good gaine, and presently carried beyond the Seas to a second profite, and yet the mischefe ends not here: for by this means the takers vp of money in forraine Countreys must necessarily driue a Trade to those places, from whence they draw their moneys; and so doe fill vs vp with forraine Commodities without the vent of our owne wares, but for this great euill, there is an easie remedie, and so I come to handle the next cause which is neglect of Dutie.

Forraine wares brought in with our ready moneys caryed out of this Realme.

Neither is it my intent to write of Duties in their seuerall kindes; but onely of that kinde of duty which is here thought to bee neglected by some men in their seuerall vocations. As it might peraduenture come to passe, in those who haue the working of his Maiesties coyne, either gold or siluer: if diligent care be not had in the size of euery seuerall peece, to answer iustly to his weight: for howsoeuer vpon triall of many peeces altogether, the weight may bee found according to the couenants, and within the remedies ordained in the Indenture: Yet notwithstanding many of those peeces may be sized too light, & others as much too heauy; which giueth the greater aduantage to some people, to carry away that which is ouer-weight, and so to leau

The third cause concerneth neglect of duties.

Our heauy money is conueyed beyond the seas, and melted downe into plate here in the realme.

leaue vs them which are too light, if they leaue vs any.

And this mischiefe is not single; for thereby also some Goldsmiths, regarding profit more then dutie, may bee the more readily drawne to melt downe the heauy Coyne into Plate and other ornaments both of gold and siluer.

But what might wee thinke of those men who are placed in authoritie and office for his Maiestie, if they should not with all dutifull care discharge their trust concerning that excellent Statute, wherein it is ordered, that all the moneys receiued by strangers for their Merchandise, shall be employed vpon the commodities of this Realme? the due performance whereof would not onely preuent the carrying away of much gold and siluer, but also be a meanes of greater vent of our owne wares: whereof I purpose to write something more in the next part which concerneth our commerce with strangers.

And now I come to the last point, which I feare is not the least amongst the causes of our want of money (so farre as any such may bee:) and let it not seeme strange to any man, that Trades should hurt and impouerish a Commonwealth, since it hath beene alwayes accompted an excellent means to helpe and enrich the same: for, as this truth cannot be denyed with reason, so it is likewise most certain, that the vnskilfull managing thereof hath euer prooued a great decay vnto those nations who haue been entangled with such errors. And are not the

Anno 17. Edw. 4.

The fourth cause concerneth our cō-merce with strangers.

Vnskilfull Merchants ouerthrow our Trades.

the examples too frequent in many of our owne Merchants, who not onely by the perils of the Seas and such like misfortunes, lose their goods, but also euen through want of knowledge, wisely to direct their affaires, doe ouerthrow their whole estates: neither may we properly call this their losse, but rather the kingdomes losse in them. Wherefore it were to be wished, that this mysterie of Merchandising might be left only to them, who haue had an education thereunto; and not to be vndertaken by such, who leauing their proper vocations, doe for want of skill in this, both ouerthrow themselues & others who are better practised.

But there is yet a farre greater mischiefe by our Trades beyond the Seas, when peraduenture, there might be imported yearely a greater value in forraine wares, then by any way or meanes we doe export of our owne commodities; which cannot otherwise come to passe, then with a manifest impouerishing of the Commonwealth; for as it is a certain cause to make vs rich, both in stock & treasure, when we shall carry out a greater value of our owne goods then we bring in of forrain wares; so by consequence, a course contrary to this, must of necessitie worke a contrary effect.

Neither is this importation meant otherwise then concerning those wares, which are consumed in this Realme: for the commodities which are brought in, & after carried out vnto forren parts again, canot hurt but doe greatly help the commonwealth, by encrease of his Maiesties Customes and Trades, with other imploy-

Merchants by education are onely fit to trade in forren parts.

How rich commonwealths may become poore.

Forrain wares brought in for Transito cannot hurt, but greatly helpe the commonwealth.

employments of the subiects; by which particulars I might yet set foorth the glory of the *East India* Trade, which hath brought into this Realme in fifteene moneths space, not onely so much Spice, as hath serued the same for the sayd time; but also by the superfluitie thereof, there hath beene exported into forraine parts for about 215000. pounds sterling. So then let all men iudge. for what a great value wee may hope hereafter to export yearely: when vnto these spices we may (by Gods assistance) add the infinite worth of Raw-silkes, Indicos, Callicoes, and some other things: All which are to bee issued in the nature of Cloth, Lead, Tinne, or any of our owne Merchandize to the enriching of this Kingdome by encrease of the Common-stocke. So then to conclude this poynt, we ought not to auoid the importation of forraine wares, but rather willingly to bridle our owne affections to the moderate consuming of the same: for otherwise, howsoeuer the *East India* Trade in particular is an excellent meanes greatly to encrease the stocke of mony which we send thither yearely, by returning home fiue times the value thereof in rich commodities, all which (in short time) may bee conuerted into Treasure, as is plainly shewd already in Page 25. Yet notwithstanding, if these *Indian* wares thusbrought home, cannot be spared to serue for that purpose of Treasure; but must be sent forth together with our owne natiue commodities: and yet all little enough to prouide our excesse and extraordinary consume of forraine wares: then is it likewise as certaine that

the

Hopes to increase Trade by exportation of Indian wares to forrain parts

The particular Trade to the East Indies wil bring great store of treasure into this Realme, if the generall Trade of this kingdome doe not hinder and consume it

the generall Trade of this Kingdome doth hinder and diuert the comming in of the said Treasure, by ouer-ballancing the value of our wares exported; with the importation and immoderate consume of forraine Commodities.

Therefore, forasmuch as the number of the people in this Realme, are thought to be greatly increased of late time (both in themselues and strangers) whereby necessarily the Commodities of this Kingdome, and also forraine wares, are the more consumed and wasted, a double meanes to abate the Common-wealth;) it therefore concerneth vs all in generall, and euery man in his particular, to stirre vp our minds, and diligence, to helpe the naturall Commodities of this Realme by industrie, and increase of Arts; seeing that the materials cannot bee wanting to make such Stuffes, and other things as are daily brought vnto vs from forraine parts, to the great aduantage of Strangers, and to our no lesse dammage. Neither should we neglect the riches which our Seas affoord, whilest other Nations by their labour doe procure themselues great Treasure from the same. And as the diligent performance of these things, would plentifully maintaine the poore, and much increase the common stocke of this Kingdome: so likewise for the better furtherance thereof, wee ought religiously to auoid our common excesses of food and rayment, which is growne to such a height in most degrees of people (aboue their abilitie) that it is now beyond all example of former ages. Neither is it needfull

The Dutch in particular, are said to reape such infinite wealth yearely by this fishing Trade, that without more certain knowledge thereof I dare not set downe the sum, it seemeth so vncredible.

needfull for me, to set downe the particulars of these abuses ; for they are too well knowne : and I am confident, that the wisedome of our Gouernment doth endeuour to see them as well amended, to the glorie of God, the honour of the King, and the good of the Common-
wealth. *Amen.*

FINIS.